20 FUN FACTS ABOUT WESTWARD EXPANSION

By Joan Stoltman

Gareth Stevens
PUBLISHING

Please visit our website, www.garethstevens.com. For a free color catalog of all our high-quality books, call toll free 1-800-542-2595 or fax 1-877-542-2596.

Cataloging-in-Publication Data

Names: Stoltman, Joan.
Title: 20 fun facts about westward expansion / Joan Stoltman.
Description: New York : Gareth Stevens Publishing, 2019. | Series: Fun fact file: US history! | Includes glossary and index.
Identifiers: LCCN ISBN 9781538219195 (pbk.) | ISBN 9781538219218 (library bound) | ISBN 9781538219201 (6 pack)
Subjects: LCSH: United States–Territorial expansion–Juvenile literature. | West (U.S.)–History–Juvenile literature. | West (U.S.)–Discovery and exploration–Juvenile literature.
Classification: LCC E179.5 S76 2019 | DDC 978–dc23

Published in 2019 by
Gareth Stevens Publishing
111 East 14th Street, Suite 349
New York, NY 10003

Copyright © 2019 Gareth Stevens Publishing

Designer: Sarah Liddell
Editor: Mariel Bard

Photo credits: Cover, p. 1 MPI/Stringer/Archive Photos/Getty Images; p. 5 SuperStock/SuperStock/Getty Images; p. 6 Tm/Wikimedia Commons; p. 7 Munion/Wikimedia Commons; p. 8 (Louis de Onís) Thelmadatter/Wikimedia Commons; p. 8 (John Quincy Adams) ApolloFirenze/Wikimedia Commons; p. 9 Dr. Alan Lipkin/Shutterstock.com; p. 10 Morphart Creation/Shutterstock.com; pp. 11, 22, 24 Everett Historical/Shutterstock.com; p. 12 File Upload Bot (Magnus Manske)/Wikimedia Commons; p. 13 Slick-o-bot/Wikimedia Commons; p. 14 Themudmom1/Wikimedia Commons; p. 15 Photoonlife/Shutterstock.com; p. 16 SteinsplitterBot/Wikimedia Commons; p. 17 Fœ/Wikimedia Commons; p. 18 Sascha Brück~commonswiki/Wikimedia Commons; p. 19 Wusel007/Wikimedia Commons; p. 20 SNEHIT/Shutterstock.com; p. 21 Bettmann/Contributor/Bettmann/Getty Images; p. 23 Tryphon/Wikimedia Commons; p. 25 L. Erin/Shutterstock.com; p. 26 MPF/Wikimedia Commons; p. 27 AndreasPraefcke/Wikimedia Commons; p. 29 Alonso de Mendoza/Wikimedia Commons.

Printed in the United States of America

CPSIA compliance information: Batch #CS18GS: For further information contact Gareth Stevens, New York, New York at 1-800-542-2595.

Contents

Words in the glossary appear in **bold** type the first time they are used in the text.

A Growing Nation

America is a lot bigger than it used to be! After winning independence from the British, the country's first official borders were set in 1783 by the **Treaty** of Paris. After that, the United States continued to grow as people bought and fought for more land across the North American **continent**.

Americans believed they had a duty to spread the country all the way to the Pacific Ocean. This belief was called Manifest Destiny, and it was a major **goal** of the US government, especially during the 1800s. During this time, the country **expanded** westward, as well as to the north and south.

In 1845, newspaper editor John L. O'Sullivan came up with the term "Manifest Destiny" for why the government felt it had to expand the country.

FACT 1

The Louisiana Purchase almost doubled the size of the country!

The United States' territory stopped at the Mississippi River until President Thomas Jefferson made the first big land buy of westward expansion. France sold this huge chunk of land to the United States in 1803 for only $15 million—about four cents an **acre**. That's like buying a football field for around a nickel!

The Louisiana Purchase

The Louisiana Purchase was about 828,000 square miles (2,144,510 sq km). Today, all or part of 15 states are found in what was the Louisiana Purchase!

Spain didn't get any money for giving Florida to the United States under the Transcontinental Treaty of 1819!

Instead, the United States agreed to cover $5 million of

damage caused by a fight **John Quincy Adams**   **Luis de Onís**

between the Americans

and the Spanish in

Florida. The United

States also claimed

the Oregon Territory

and gained land along

the Louisiana Purchase.

The Transcontinental Treaty is also called the Adams-Onís Treaty. It's named for the men who made the deal: American secretary of state John Quincy Adams and Spanish minister to the United States Luis de Onís.

FACT 3

The land bought with the Treaty of Guadalupe Hidalgo includes a point where four states all meet!

Signed on February 2, 1848, the treaty ended the Mexican-American War. It also gave more than 525,000 square miles (1.4 million sq km) of land to the United States for $15 million.

FACT 4

Thomas Jefferson thought mastodons roamed the West!

People had no idea who or what lived in the West, so President Jefferson sent **explorers** to check it out. This included the famous **expedition** by Meriwether Lewis and William Clark in 1804 to the Louisiana Purchase and Oregon Territory.

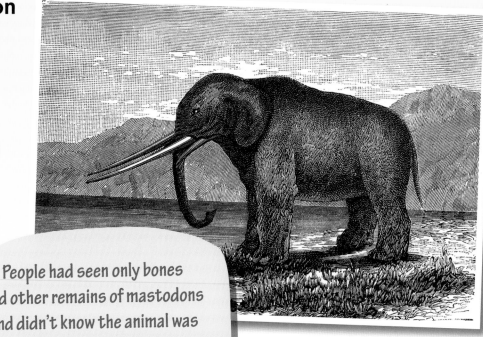

People had seen only bones and other remains of mastodons and didn't know the animal was **extinct** by this time.

FACT 5

A baby boy traveled with Lewis and Clark!

He started the trip at just 2 months old, and his mother, Sacagawea, carried him on her back. Sacagawea was a Native American from the Shoshone tribe. She helped guide Lewis and Clark's group and taught them about plants, roots, and berries they could eat or use for medicine.

Hundreds of living things were either discovered or written about in detail for the first time during explorations of the West.

FACT 6

Lewis and Clark sent President Jefferson a live "barking squirrel" from their expedition!

In their journals, the men called prairie dogs "barking squirrels." Lewis and Clark saw and sketched many creatures, including grizzly bears, western hognose snakes, and black-tailed prairie dogs, during their expedition.

FACT 7

Artists' paintings of the West were the first color pictures of these new territories and the people who lived there!

In the 1830s, George Catlin traveled with and painted pictures of different Native American groups. Thomas Moran painted beautiful **landscapes**, including pictures of what would become Yellowstone National Park.

FACT 8

The Oregon Trail wasn't the only way west!

During the 1840s and 1850s, hundreds of thousands of people used different trails to get to new lands. Many left their homes in search of a better life after struggling to make enough money back east.

Some people wanted to own property out west, and some wanted to farm new land. Others were looking for gold!

Trails to the West!

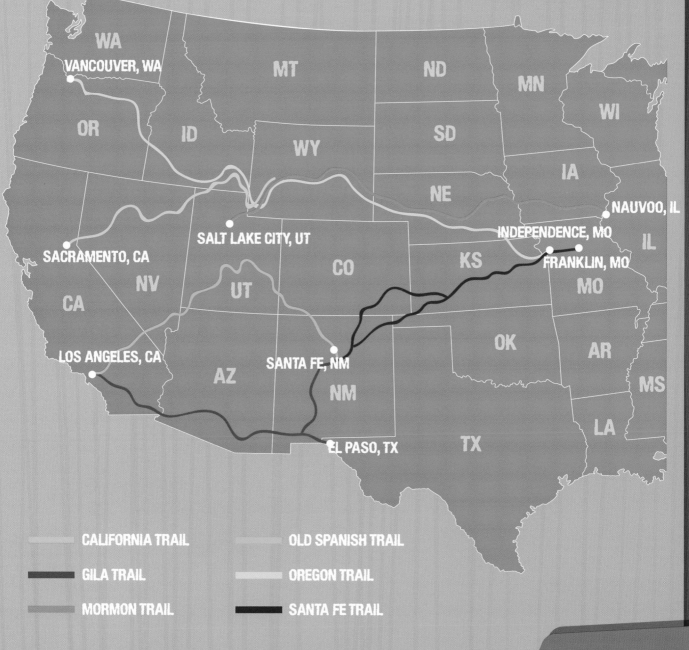

WA — VANCOUVER, WA

MT

ND

MN

WI

OR

ID

WY

SD

IA

NE

NAUVOO, IL

SALT LAKE CITY, UT

INDEPENDENCE, MO

IL

SACRAMENTO, CA

NV

UT

CO

KS

FRANKLIN, MO

MO

CA

LOS ANGELES, CA

AZ

SANTA FE, NM

NM

OK

AR

MS

TX

LA

EL PASO, TX

CALIFORNIA TRAIL   OLD SPANISH TRAIL

GILA TRAIL   OREGON TRAIL

MORMON TRAIL   SANTA FE TRAIL

The ride along the trails west was so bumpy, milk could be turned into butter!

Some people traveled in wagons called prairie schooners, which were lighter and smaller than Conestoga wagons used in the East. But prairie schooners didn't have springs to cushion bumps like bigger wagons, so milk hanging in buckets underneath them was churned into butter!

The wagons filled up fast with about 2,000 pounds (907 kg) of supplies.

Buffalo chips were especially handy in the Great Plains, where most of the land is flat and grassy rather than wooded.

FACT 10

People cooked over fires made using buffalo poop!

If travelers couldn't find wood to burn, they used pieces of dried buffalo poop, called "chips." Buffalo chips burn well because they're mostly grass! Children would run around and gather up chips for the day's fires.

Left Behind

Thousands of pioneers carved their names into rocks along the trails!

Independence Rock in the Wyoming Territory was a popular camping stop. Before leaving for the next part of their trip, some people added their names or a message to the rock. Even after more than 150 years, many names are still there!

These are names of pioneers heading west. A pioneer is someone who is the first to explore a new area.

FACT 12

Wheel marks from wagons traveling the Oregon Trail can still be seen today!

With more than 400,000 people using the trails from about 1840 to 1880, the roads were constantly in use. Over time, the wagon wheels wore down the dirt or rock, leaving marks in the ground called ruts.

People often packed too much and had to dump supplies along the trail!

To lighten the loads of the wagons, "leeverites" (as in "leave 'er right here") were **discarded** along the trails. Tossed items included clothes, shoes, tents, furniture, and even bacon!

wagon left behind

Some people would take to the trails and collect leeverites so they could resell them!

For the Taking!

The Homestead Act of 1862 granted 1.6 million land claims!

A homestead is a piece of land given away by the government. By paying $18 in fees and promising to live on and improve the land for 5 years, any American—including women and former slaves—could claim land!

The Homestead Act officially ended in 1976, but the last homestead was recognized in Alaska in 1988.

Rumor had it that the government had set aside the state of Kansas for former slaves only!

Even though the rumor wasn't true, a lot of people moved there to start a new life. In 1879 alone, more than 6,000 former slaves left the South and settled in Kansas.

An exodus is when a lot of people leave at once. Former slaves who left the South for Kansas were called exodusters.

The land homesteaders rushed to claim had actually been settled by Native Americans who were forced off their lands by the US government years earlier.

People called "sooners" hid in bushes so they could grab the best land first!

The Oklahoma Territory was ready to be given to homesteaders at noon on April 22, 1889. But some people broke the rules, got there early, and hid on the best plots of land. Oklahoma has been called the Sooner State ever since.

FACT 17

Texas was an independent republic before it became a state!

In 1836, Texas declared independence from Mexico, complete with its own government and president. Then on December 29, 1845, Texas became the 28th US state.

Sam Houston was elected president of Texas. The city of Houston is named after him!

In 1859 alone, more than 50,000 people traveled to Pikes Peak in search of gold. The mountain is named for Zebulon Pike, one of Thomas Jefferson's explorers!

FACT 18

California wasn't the only state to have a gold rush, but its rush was the biggest!

A flood of people came to California looking for gold, which helped it become a state in 1850. Other gold rushes of the 1800s happened at Pikes Peak in Colorado, Black Hills in South Dakota, and South Pass in Wyoming.

FACT 19

Alaska used to be a Russian colony!

America purchased Alaska from Russia in 1867, but few Americans settled there at first. In the 1880s, Alaska's population boomed as mining and fishing became popular there. In 1959, Alaska became the 49th US state.

Two companies worked to build a transcontinental railroad to link the East and West Coasts!

The Union Pacific Railroad Company started laying track near Omaha, Nebraska. The Central Pacific Railroad Company started in Sacramento, California. The two sets of tracks met in Utah on May 10, 1869.

Now people could travel by train and get to the West in just a few days instead of walking on trails alongside wagons for months.

From Sea to Shining Sea

Westward expansion officially ended on February 14, 1912, when Arizona became a state—the last of the 48 contiguous, or connected, states. America had accomplished its goal of Manifest Destiny, stretching across all of North America!

What was once unknown territory became a place where people could try building a better life and accomplishing their own goals. Would you have been willing to make the difficult journey from sea to shining sea?

This famous painting shows a woman leading Americans west. Behind her, settlers, gold seekers, and farmers follow on foot, by wagon, or by train toward new land.

Glossary

acre: a unit of measurement for land that is equal to 43,560 square feet (4,047 sq m)

continent: one of Earth's seven great landmasses

damage: harm that is done to something or someone

discard: to get rid of

expand: to get larger in size

expedition: a trip made for a certain purpose

explorer: a person who searches in order to find out new things

extinct: no longer existing or living

goal: something important someone wants to do

landscape: a picture of a natural scene outdoors

republic: a form of government in which the people elect representatives who run the government

transcontinental: going across a continent

treaty: a government agreement between countries

For More Information

Books

Collins, Terry. *Into the West: Causes and Effects of U.S. Westward Expansion.* North Mankato, MN: Capstone Press, 2014.

Machajewski, Sarah. *A Kid's Life During the Westward Expansion.* New York, NY: PowerKids Press, 2015.

Otfinoski, Steven. *A Primary Source History of Westward Expansion.* North Mankato, MN: Capstone Press, 2015.

Yasuda, Anita. *Westward Expansion of the United States, 1801–1861.* Minneapolis, MN: Core Library, 2014.

Websites

All About the Oregon Trail
oregontrail101.com/allabout.html
Read this fun online book about the Oregon Trail.

Lewis and Clark: The Journey Begins
teacher.scholastic.com/activities/lewis_clark/prepare.htm
Follow Lewis and Clark's journey!

Index